The Road To Armageddon

- A Free Spiritual Guide -

With Illustrations By

Zaza Wouters & Justin Brunelle

Edited By Chuck Facas

Copyright 2012 Chuck Facas

Cover design by Aki Fujiyoshi

ISBN: 978-0-9851919-1-7

FEATURING

Marilynn Hughes (MH)

Pastor Howard Storm (PS)

Imam Dr. Salahuddin M. Muhammad (MUH)

Robert Thurman (THU)

Reverend Monsignor James Moroney (MM)

Francis X. Clooney, S.J. (CL)

Reverend Caroline Stacey (STA)

John Zaffis (JZ)

Rabbi Mitchell M. Hurvitz (RM)

===================================

===================================

Mystical experience goes beyond ordinary sense perception - revealing deeper truths about ourselves and our relationship with the divine.

Mystics have been ridiculed, persecuted and even killed for their beliefs - but their teachings endure, urging us to look beyond the ordinary...

...and into the eyes of God.

===================================

===================================

I can't always explain my experiences in relation to the dogmas or doctrines of every faith, but... as bad as some of these demons are, which they are very, very serious and they are, by far, so rabid in this world. It's almost impossible to even explain. One night I was given to go over a particular US city and the entire upper atmosphere was filled with so many demons it was almost impossible to get through it - and when I got through it I was exhausted for like two weeks - and it was a particular city where there was just really dominantly dark at that point - and so we have to recognize that much of what we believe to be true really isn't. There is more to what we're doing here than what we maybe want to deal with. MH 1 (1:02) (1:00 seconds)

===

The Road To Armageddon

===

I believe that this world that we're experiencing is, to put it kindly, small potatoes. It's like a little experience that God has given us for our benefit and edification and our spiritual development. This is not graduate school by any means. It's more like nursery school. When I asked Jesus, "Is this like elementary school?" He said no. And I said, "Kindergarten?" He goes no. And I said, "Nursery school?" And He says, "Mmm, like nursery school." The lessons of this world are avoid evil and love good; be kind to one another - these are not really difficult or intellectually challenging lessons that were learning down here and which plenty of people are failing to learn. (2:15) PS (53 seconds)

It's possible that if you are not progressing properly in this realm that you could go backwards - but that's usually for people who are engaging in seriously destructive things. Dominantly dark and evil would be people who are engaging in murder, rape - serious, serious acts against life - because the way energy is perceived in the mystical realms is acts for or against life - and so to go into the dominantly dark and evil realms you would have to do some pretty bad stuff. However, just having the issues of vanity and lust could put you in a lower realm. (1:08) MH (46 seconds)

===

===

This is just a small portion of what I was shown - it's called the universal sphere of realms. We are in here - this is the third realm; and this is the fourth realm - this fourth realm is the astral plane. This third realm would be a third dimensional reality which we reside on. In the very center is the first realm which, as you can see, is totally black - that's total darkness, that's where pure evil resides. The second realm is where dominant darkness resides.

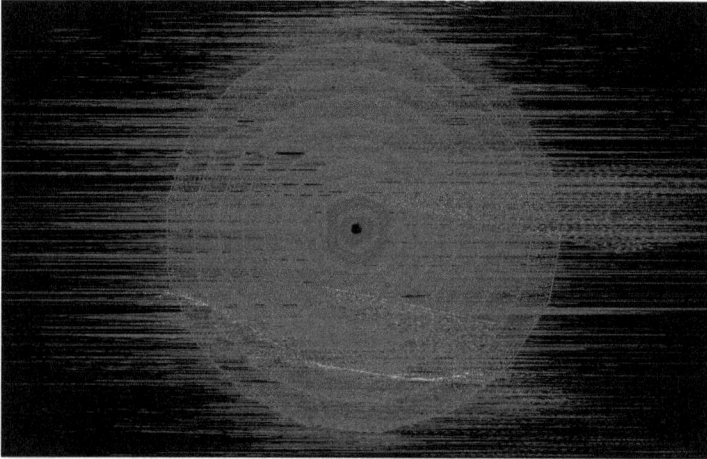

When you're dealing with realms one and two, you're dealing with purgatories and hell realms - both of these are even lower realms than we are - and when you're dealing with three and four you're dealing with purgatories and people who are trying to reach beyond into realms five and above, which go out into higher and higher gradations of light.

But these four realms together make up what is called the border worlds - the underworlds - and so the reason why this is important is because if you understand this is where we are - and God is somewhere way out there - then what I'm going to try to describe and explain makes a lot more sense. (1:04) MH (1:06 seconds)

When we die, we human beings have no power to ascend or descend spiritually. We are taken by guides - who could be either angels or demons - to what we carry in our hearts. If we carry hate in our hearts we go to a world hate - and if we carry love in our hearts we're carried to world of love. (2:06) PS (31 seconds)

It's not good enough just to be nice, to speak nicely and have a seething mind filled with eros and thanatos. Because when you die, it's that seething mind that will carry your spiritual gene into places where seething beings live - and you don't want to go in seething places. (2:42) TH (16 seconds)

In the mystical realms you see what is called the energetic truth about a person or another being or a spirit. In the physical realm we can all disguise ourselves in any way that we choose - we can be a wolf in sheep's clothing in the physical realm. But when you're in the mystical realm what you really are is what people see. MH1 (5:45) (24 seconds)

And there's no deception and there's no fooling around - you can't get out of it. You can say, "I don't want this." Well, that ain't going to do you any good because you spent your whole life building your heart. What we are doing here in this world is building a heart of love, or building a heart that's not love. (2:07) PS (22 seconds)

We have to become more like God in order to go to a higher place. We go where we're compatible - as depressing as that may be. (1:09) MH (12 seconds)

===================================

"You will know the truth and the truth

will set you free."

John 8:32

===================================

I remember many times that the Angels would show me, "How would you save a world that serves its function to perfection?" And I would say, "What you do mean?" And they would say, "The mortal realms are where the battles between good and evil rage - they rage around you, they rage inside of you. This world is functioning to perfection." The purpose of being in a mortal realm is to become aware of that interior process that has to begin - of purification - and that's when we start understanding... we understand that the goal is God. (1:22) MH (39 seconds)

If you leave your mind filled with unconscious drives of greed and hatred, eros and thanatos, then they will drive you into bad life forms. So the whole goal in a contemplative culture is to go into the unconscious and become conscious of it, and to cleanse yourself of the negative, ego-centered, ignorance-dominated drives. Like "I want this" or "I hate that." (2:42) TH (22 seconds)

Why is it so important to purify the soul? Because that's the true you; that's who you are. Most people get caught up with how they look, or they look at the vehicle that carries the self. It's just like the person who wants to get a nice body. They go to Gold's Gym and they lift the weights and they do the push-ups and the sit-ups and all these kinds of things. So now, you do all of that so that you can have a beautiful body, and what do you do for the inside? So there's work that you have to do on the inside so that you can make sure that you get rid of those vices. (3:43) MUH (33 seconds)

One of the things I've learned in the spiritual realms is that a thought of vice is actually what gives dominion for a demon of that vice to come in and be around you. So let's say you have a greedy thought - that is enough grounds for a demon to come around and start suggesting things to you. If you have the opposite thought where you want to be charitable to somebody - that also gives the same permission for an angel of that virtue to come in and be around you, as well. And this is where you begin understanding the battle that goes on around us. (1:20) MH (41 seconds)

We've all seen these movies in which you've got a good angel and a demon sitting on someone's shoulders saying, "Go ahead and do this, no, go ahead and do that," pulling the dark side and the bright side of us sort of thing. It's the truth. As we sit here right now there are myriads of angels and myriads of demons - there's light and darkness that's constantly vying for our soul. (MM) (28 seconds)

The best way to always describe what a demon is - is something that was cast out, tossed down here on earth - into hell, the pit, whatever you want to call it - and it's to wreak havoc, to undo everything on a positive level; to be able to break down people, to break down their life structures and to do things on a totally negative level. (3:12) JZ (22 seconds)

In order to begin purifying and begin getting rid of some of our vices, we have to start behaving differently and thinking differently - because if you understand that when you have a simple thought of greed or a simple thought of vanity, you're giving dominion for a dark force to be around you and influencing your thoughts - then you become more and more aware of how much more vigilance you have to keep over your mind, heart, and soul so that you are progressing. (1:24) MH (32 seconds)

Those that want to change have to first change the way they think. If you don't change it - you can dress up a certain way and it seems like everything is okay - a person could, even a Muslim, he can learn so many verses from the Koran, he can stop eating pork, he can fast in the month of Ramadan - but if he or she have not changed the way they think, then their behaviour is going to be the same. They might camouflage it for a while, but then when they get back into the environment, the same thinking is there - so the behaviour is going to come right back. (3:44) MUH (34 seconds)

=======================================

"We know that we are of God

and the world is in the power of the evil one."

Catechism of the Catholic Church

=======================================

St. Francis was gathered in the field with some of his brothers right outside of a small-town in Umbria and there was a fellow who had the ability to see demons.

And as he stood in this field he saw legions of demons as far as he could see that were lined up in the field who were just plotting as to how to tempt these Franciscan Friars.

Then he walks down the street to the entrance to the town and there's one old demon sitting there yawning, leaning back by the side of the entrance to the town. And he went to one of the Franciscan Friars and he said, "Brother, I've been given this gift to be able to see these things. Why are there millions of demons here with you 20 in the field and only one by the gate that's filled with all these people."

And he said, "Because all that's needed is one little old demon in order to bring those people to perdition - but the devil has to work very hard in order to tempt those who have given their lives completely to God." (MM) (1:10 seconds)

==

==

What you have to understand is that there's a continual

warfare that goes on for every soul on this earth. Much of the time when we're here on earth, we're thinking all the battles between good and evil are going on outside of us but we don't recognize that that battle is going on inside of us as well. (1:09) MH (17 seconds)

Anything that's good, a demon or a devil will do in reverse. Now what do I mean by that? If a person is a good person and they go to church and they're trying to lead a halfway decent life - they will rebel against that, they'll try to break down that individual, wear that individual down to be able to get them to do mean, rotten types of things and create all kinds of havoc. (3:12) JZ (23 seconds)

What the forces of darkness want us to do is to spend our life trying to grab for all the gusto that we can get - to get stuff - and to get things - and to treat people like things. (MM) (15 seconds)

There really is a purpose for us being here - and the purpose is not to live a worldly life, be successful and all this stuff. The purpose has to do with this purification process that God sent us to the mortal realms to overcome - but if you think about how brilliant this is of the dark side... if the dark side can get us to focus entirely on worldly things and waste our time - works for him, doesn't it? Because we waste an entire lifetime and accomplish nothing. (1:16) MH (35 seconds)

Are demons clever? They are the most sophisticated, most cunning things you could ever deal with. Why? They have the wisdom of the ages. They have the knowledge of the ages. They know how to manipulate things. They know how to trick people. They know how to do things very, very... cunning is the best way I can describe it. (3:15) JZ (22 seconds)

Usually what happens when people really turn their path towards God is that they will begin what will become almost a real warfare for their soul - and a lot of people are really surprised by this. But as long as we're kind of content and lackadaisical about just living life and not doing anything - the demons and Satan already has dominion over us, so they don't have to make themselves known. But when we turn away and we start saying, "We want God," then they have to fight for us. MH (37 seconds)

The more spiritual an individual is, the more they pray, the more that they are into their belief system, the more of a target that individual actually can be. Because trying to win a very spiritual individual over - no matter what denomination you're talking about - that's like the grand prize. JZ (21 seconds)

But you have to push through this warfare - you cannot back down - because that's their goal - is that they want to wear you down so you're so tired you're like, "This is too hard - I'm just going to go back to my lackadaisical lifestyle - nothing bothered me then." (1:10) MH (14 seconds)

I think it's probably wise to admit this about ourselves and our society that evil is real - people are not always going to be good or do good. And to be open to the idea that some of those forces of evil – just as the forces of good – may be invisible, and that whether one calls it a devil or not is maybe less important than realizing that there are evils that we cannot see, evils that are spiritual that we only partially grasp, and we should be humbled before reality - that we don't control the good, we don't control the evil, and there may be forces around us that can hurt us and help us and we have to find our way between them. CL (40:00) (38 seconds)

The most powerful thing against the demons in any of the spheres is - I'm getting say something that the exorcists usually say - which is confession. The sacrament of confession is, according to many exorcists, more powerful than the rite of exorcism - but in my experience in the mystical realms... the reason that's the case is because by confessing your sins, you are taking away the dominion that they have. They have dominion because of your agreement to certain sins or vices or ways of thinking. (1:19) MH (33 seconds)

You are your catalyst. That's the best way I can describe that to you. You are in control of your vessel. You have to fight back. You have to protect yourself. And the way I recommend to anybody is… I don't care if you worship a 5-pound quartz crystal - I don't care what it is - as long as it's on a positive. You call upon that positive to be able to help protect yourself - and you have to fight back. (3:07) JZ (28 seconds)

==

The Lord Demon

==

In regards to some of the demons associated with the deadly sins, there is a demon of rage...

...and it's interesting because the demon of rage operates and appears very much like a person who has an uncontrollable rage issue. It's a small little snake - and you can see it in the mystical realm - but when it becomes energized...

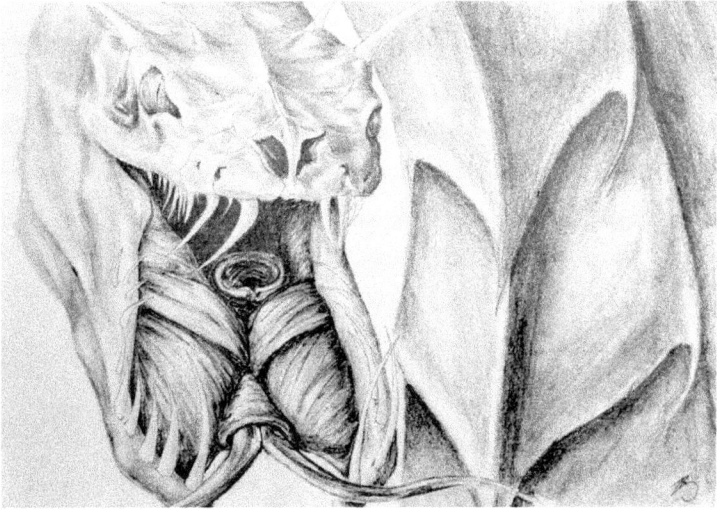

...it becomes huge, red, pumping with fury - and you've got to get out of its way. And so that's one of the demons of rage. (35 seconds)

=====================================

=====================================

Narcissism - which is an aspect of pride - and a lot of these things are offshoots of the deadly sins - but like narcissism in particular there's a demon called Gold Eyes.

He's a very frightening demon. When he is inside the soul
of a person he will appear as this gold light coming
through their eyes and he's so enraged - and it's an
imperialistic rage.

It's like the rage that you would see from someone who feels very entitled.

When you get this creature to come out it's like a big raging wall of fire - and that's narcissism and imperialistic rage. (39 seconds)

===================================

===================================

The Gull demon is a demon of destructive sexuality. The worst ones - which would be the incubus and the succubus - these are much more higher caliber demons, they have a lot more strength and they can do a lot more damage to a soul. These have to do with lust.

You'll see them as very attractive...

...but when they reveal themselves they're like a skeleton with flesh hanging from it, spider webs - almost like a corpse that's been decomposing. You know how it says in the scriptures somewhere: "Outside they look one way and inside they're like a ravening wolf."

That's the way the demonic is. (38 seconds)

==

==

One of the most important and most disturbing demons to mention is called the Lord Demon - and one of the reasons it's so disturbing is because of its commonality. Christ showed me this demon and I was so overwhelmed by the power of this demon - and then He showed me that… it was a real, real mortal battle to the death kind of thing. I mean, this demon was really sneaky.

The Lord Demon represents, more than anything, self-intelligence - so you have to have the ego, you have to have the greed - and the avarice is anger that's disordered. The Lord Demon is the most common demon in the world today because we're so smart as human beings - we're so self-intelligent - that we're smarter than God, right? (55 seconds)

We want the opinion of God - the opinion of the prophets, saints, mystics and sages from all time - to be of equal value to every single one of us down here below. But in reality, it's not. (17 seconds)

If you have to hold on to the self-intelligence that, "I'm right. This whole concept of demons is illogical. The concept that God would not just love all His creatures no matter what is illogical," then you're going to be visiting with the Lord Demon. And the Lord Demon, Jesus Christ also told me, was the most common cause of damnation today. (29 seconds)

And that's interesting because in Fatima in 1917, when the Blessed Virgin appeared to the three shepherd children, she had said the most common reason for souls to go to hell at that time was sins of impurity. But our society has become so arrogant that we have become smarter than God. (23 seconds)

Think about that. Think about us down here in the third and fourth realm - and God somewhere ad infinitum - and we believe that. That's not going to allow us to grow. (12 seconds)

And the Lord Demon is so sneaky - all he has to do is convince you that it's illogical: Religion is illogical; the moral code is illogical; the Ten Commandments are illogical. (12 seconds)

But if we think that we're smarter than the simple moral code - we think that anything can be changed according to our simple whims - we become really vulnerable to having a voice speaking inside of us telling us we're right - and it gets harder and harder to get away from this one because the Lord Demon is really, really powerful.

This is not like some little pansy demon. This Lord Demon is a scary creature - and he will come to you and when you see him in the mystical - when he becomes his true self - his teeth are all pointy, he turns red and black and blood oozes from his pores and his teeth, and there's flesh on his teeth. He's the most disgusting creature you'll ever see - but, boy, is he good at what he does. MH (55 seconds)

======================================

"If I ascend into heaven, You are there:

If I make my bed in hell, behold, You are there."

Psalm 139:8

======================================

Before my experience with Jesus I was a successful, A+, American guy, who believed that it's a dog-eat-dog world - life is about competition and winning and not being a loser - life is about not being the victim but being the aggressor - and I tried to bully my way in my relationships. I tried to intimidate people. I didn't hesitate to physically assault people and verbally assault them. I did very well - I got I got promotions, I got money, I got prestige, I got honors - I was a winner. I was very aggressive with my wife, with my children. A lot of people despised me and I was glad of it because I figured part of the quality of being a winner was that there were casualties in your relationships along the way. And my friends were people that subscribed to the same sort of them highly assertive, self-centered, narcissistic, point of view.

I believe that there is no such thing as an atheist - I believe that everybody has a God - the only question is, "Who's your god?" And for atheists, their god is themselves. So they have these little bitty gods, which is their self, and that was me and my friends - we were all in love with ourselves and that's who we worshipped.

Having yourself as a God fails in a crisis because you have nobody to turn to because you can't do anything about the circumstances - they're just collapsing around you. (1:43 seconds)

I was dying in a hospital - and it was catastrophic - and you have nothing left but hopelessness and despair and a very fatalistic, nihilistic view of the world - that life sucks and then you die and who cares. Which is pretty bleak when you think about it. And that's what I was believing when I died on June 1, 1985 at 38 years old. (29 seconds)

Your consciousness - when you die - doesn't cease. That's the interesting thing is that consciousness survives bodily death. And so when you have a negative consciousness you get to go into negative world - the world where 'of like' people and like consciousness - and it's a very cruel and brutal and horrible place.

It was much like what has been described as rats when they over-reproduce in too small a cage and they just start gnawing on each other. That's what they were doing - basically people biting, tearing, ripping each other apart continuously. (PS) (44 seconds)

==

==

One of the things as a priest - I've been a priest for 31 years - and one of the things that is the most wonderful moment in the day is when at 2:30 in the morning you get a call to go to the hospital and somebody's dying. At first you grumble that it's 2:30 in the morning - I got this 7 o'clock mass tomorrow, I'm going to be tired all day, and you whine about that - and then you get up and you go to the hospital. But when you're standing by that bed, and you look at everybody standing around it, life is clearer and makes more sense at that moment than it does any other time during the day. Because at that moment there's no one who dies saying, "I wish I'd gotten more stuff. I wish I'd committed more sin. I wish I'd been more selfish." They all die saying, "I wish I'd loved more." (MM) (59 seconds)

==

==

I thought about my life - and as I thought about my life I realized - since I'd been a teacher all my life - that somehow I'd missed the whole point; that whatever the point of life was not only had I missed it but I failed it. I'd failed to recognize what the course was about and I was clueless and whatever I was supposed to have achieved I didn't achieve it because I ended up in this cesspool - this horrible cesspool - and so obviously I was a big failure. (2:09) PS (31 seconds)

One of the beautiful things about Hindu tradition is that God is very, very accommodating and God is very open to adjustment - and whatever way a human being happens to be heading or wandering, God is able to go there and meet the person there. The example is given in some scriptures that if we are seeking God in a very basic way, we're like little children running around in the courtyard and God is like our mother who will find us wherever we are, both to protect us from harm and to make us well. (3:18) CL (31 seconds)

We can trust that God's love and mercy will overcome our sinfulness. And that's true whether we're the worst sinner in the world or whether we've actually led a pretty decent God-fearing upright life of kindness and mercy and compassion. That God's grace is what brings us into a right relationship with Him in the last analysis. Yes, we respond by good works and so on and so forth, and all we have to do is simply acknowledge that we need that grace. STC (8:00) (30 seconds)

After the people in darkness had devastated me and emotionally, psychologically, spiritually had torn me down to nothing - I heard my voice say, "Pray to God." And I thought - I don't pray, I don't believe in God. That's what I thought. And the voice said, "Pray to God." And I thought - I don't know how to pray, I don't pray. And the voice said, "Pray to God." And I thought - I used to pray, I knew how to pray once! (2:10) PS (37 seconds)

No matter where we are - the second a soul wants God...
God comes - just like that! It's amazing to me because to
me that demonstrates mercy - that's what love and mercy
is - and that's the corrective, merciful love of God.
Because every single one of these people - and many of
these people have written to me - who've had these
experiences to hell and have called out for help - have
been so blown away by that merciful nature of God their
entire life changes. (1:39) MH (32 seconds)

There is in the universe a caring, a love, a compassion -
some kind of meaning to the universe and I called out to
that and I said, "Jesus please save me." And with that, He
- Jesus - the being of light, the ambassador of God, came
over me and loved me and took me out of that place. And
that changed everything and my whole life - my entire
life for the past 25 years - has all been about that moment
and trying to get people to say, "God I need you, Jesus I
need you, Allah help me." However they can express it.
(2:10) PS (41 seconds)

If we put our reliance back towards where it should be -
which is on God - and we don't make ourselves our own
gods - we humble ourselves and let God lovingly correct
us and bring us through that path of purification... He
will! He will not leave you behind. The only time people
are left where they are is because they really, truly,
honestly want to be there - and that's one of the hardest
things for people to understand is that you stay there
because you don't want to do anything different - you like
it the way things are - you're compatible to it! (1:46) MH
(38 seconds)

```
================================================
```

"And he begins a new life

with the wisdom of a former life;

and he begins to strive again,

ever onwards towards perfection."

Bhagavad Gita 6.43

```
================================================
```

The dogma of materialism I think arose from the dogma
of the inquisition - of the Christian Church - and burning
Giordano Bruno and muzzling Galileo Galilei and many
other lesser people - burning and muzzling. And so to
escape from that after the renaissance and reformation
and enlightenment, the thinkers and intelligentsia in
Europe went to another extreme to get away from being
dominated by the church and being threatened with hell
and so forth, and so they abandoned having a soul. They
decided we don't even have one - we're just a species, we
have genes, we have drives, survival of the fittest, and
went on through all of those different theories. And then
they got to where they... like Carl Sagan, one of his last
books was When Demons Stalked the Earth, and it had to
do with the Fundamentalists that he'd had to tangle with
in Arkansas and other places as a scientist. And the idea
was that if anything non-physical were admitted to exist
in the world, this would open the door for all kinds of
crazies and new inquisitions and demented creationists -
like the world is 7,000 years old and the Grand Canyon
was made in a flash flood and Adam was a white guy...
just a silly bunch of stuff. And then they'd end up getting
political power - these religions - and they'd start
clamping down on free thought and scientific discovery
like they did before. (2:45) TH (1:29 seconds)

Did the Garden of Eden really happen? Was the world made - the universe made in literally seven days... or six days and a day of rest? I mean, is that how it really happened - that God spoke the universe into being? And sometimes, in discourse, religious people can't get passed that - that it's real facts - into a discourse about an even deeper truth underneath which is a description of the estrangement in the human community and between human beings and God. We let the details trip us up. (3:50) STA (36 seconds)

So the dogma of materialism in a spiritual sense boils down to that view of not understanding the common sense reality and scientific viability of former and future lives - in some form - and that's the heart wrong view of our psychotic culture, which thinks it's not connected to the world, it can keep messing with the climate, it can kill off all the animals, cut all the trees, do whatever it is. The rapture people do it as a sort of warped spiritual thing, but the materialists do it because, "I'm not going to be here, so I'm going to use it up." And then they will say, "Oh, no, but I'm not unethical, I'm a humanist and I care about my children – so I'm not going to wreck the planet." But actually they are wrecking the planet. (2:48) TH (46 seconds)

If we waste the time here - if we don't take the time to purify ourselves or to move upwards then we're going to start circling - and what I mean by circling is when you see people… for those who believe in reincarnation - and I've had a lot of experiences myself - I didn't believe in the reincarnation until I started having mystical experiences about them and I've had thousands of them now - but for those who believe in reincarnation you end up coming back and doing the same thing over and over again - with the same characters, the same configuration. And until you see, "I'm doing something wrong here - there's a reason why I keep doing the same thing" - and it's made more difficult because most people don't remember their previous lives. But sometimes when people become more spiritually alert you'd be surprised how quickly they start remembering. (1:26) MH (54 seconds)

There's a very strong sense in the most ancient parts of Hinduism that we are, in fact, on a journey that takes many lifetimes. To be a being in this world is not done in a short period of time, even if that short period of time is 100 years - but that the purification of nature, the discovery of true identity comes in small packets, which we would call one lifetime or another lifetime. And in Hinduism, as in Jainism and Buddhism, there is a sense that one can be reborn again and again into new bodies as one journeys along one's path.

There is no guarantee, of course, that every body and every rebirth is better than the one before because we're really faced with the prospect of what do you do with the body you have; what do you do with the opportunities of your current life? And then, in a sense, that if we use those well, we move into a more pure, more focused bodies that are directed to the divine. And if we become distracted - if we begin to forget who we are - then we might come back in a body that is more immersed in matter and less able to be open to the divine. So, there is a way in which every life is extremely important because it really charts our way on the course - and yet every life also is simply part of a much larger journey that takes a much longer time. (3:17) CL (1:23 seconds)

There's a karmic understanding to everything which is something that's not quite correct, and there's an eternal understanding which is the real truth. And so we circle and we keep doing the same thing over because we have a karmic understanding - which doesn't create peace - it's very chaotic - we're usually messed up. Once we reach that eternal understanding there's peace. And that's one of the ways you can tell. Like when someone meets a new person, if it's an eternal thing there'll be a lot of peace. (35 seconds)

If it's karmic, there may be a lot of chaos and a lot of really intense emotions and things like that. That may very well indicate that there is an issue that's coming up from previous existences that either has to do with you and that particular person, or it's just that this particular person is going to play that role that has been played for you before in previous existences - and that's why it brings up all this intensity. But a lot of times even something that starts out karmic, if the two parties are seeking an eternal solution, it can end up well - it can become eternal - it can amend to an eternal situation if the two parties both go in that direction. (1:27) MH (48 seconds)

I think a lot of individuals can be reincarnated because there was karma carried over from a past life. And some of the traditional belief systems in that is that people keep reincarnating and reincarnating until they actually get it right. JZ (12:00) (15 seconds)

===

"Cleanliness in next to Godliness."

Rabbi Phinehas ben-Yair

===

So how does one become more spiritually alert? You do so by doing what every human being has done for the last several thousand years. If you look at the ancient sacred texts throughout history from every single world religion it's the same process: (15 seconds)

It's prayer - prayer is speaking to God; (4 seconds)

Meditation - is listening and trying to get that answer; (5 seconds)

and Spiritual Reading - which is utilizing the works of all those people who've come before us who *have* figured it out. And there are many, many people like that, (12 seconds)

from Tibet's Milarepa to Catholicism's St. Francis DeSales and St. Catherine of Siena to… Earth Store Bodhisattva was a Buddhist monk who had a similar calling that I have where he would actually go into hell realms and liberate souls. (17 seconds)

So you do the spiritual reading to form your conscience better. The more of the spiritual reading you do, the more sensitive you become to what is vice and what is a virtue. (1:31) MH (13 seconds)

If you're not putting good thoughts or good scripture in your mind and in your soul, then something else is coming in. So if you're a person who's always in front of the television, always watching violent movies or whatever the case may be - always involved with that - then your soul is being fed something but it's not being fed anything that's going to elevate you or lift you up. In order for your soul to be lifted up you have read and study and reflect and meditate on good things. (3:42) MUH (31 seconds)

The worship, the prayer, the visits to Holy sites, the reading of the books, are not to say the more we have the better off we'll be, but all of these are wisdom and advice that lead us toward letting go of the things that stand in the way. (3:26) CL (14 seconds)

=================================

"As soon as you say, 'Lord,

I don't know how to pray,'

you can be sure you've already begun."

Josemaria Escriva

=================================

Prayer is saying I want to be a part of that life in God in me and to let it more and more fill me - my conscious life - so that more and more of how I live, how I speak, how I listen, how I make choices is caught up in what God wants to do through me. (3:54) STA (20 seconds)

Just think about being in this world, where you have to make a living, and it's the hustle and bustle in life – always running, always running – and you take out five times of the day where you have this spiritual refreshment called prayer. You take a break from all that hustle and bustle. It's something that empowers you, and it's something that keeps you grounded - because you can get lost out there just going after the dollar. And then it's like - nothing else counts, nothing else matters. (3:41) MUH (31 seconds)

Prayer is a very powerful thing. I recommend it to people continuously no matter what your structure is, no matter what your belief system is. There are all sets of prayers in different belief systems out there. I recommend very strongly to people call upon that. It doesn't hurt to say prayers. It's a very positive element in our lives. JZ (25 seconds)

A lot of times we believe when we're praying that we should be answered in a certain way. But in reality, we have to remember that God knows exactly what we need at any given time, and God's purpose isn't the same as ours.

Our purpose is often very motivated by the fact that we're in denial that this is a temporary place of existence - so God is not motivated by continuing our denial about the impermanence of this life. He's motivated by what is going to give this soul the most progress spiritually at this time. And I have seen many situations where miraculous things have occurred and many other situations where the answer is no. Nobody can explain that except God because only God knows why He says yes and why He says no and why other times He says, "No, but how about this?" But it's because God has that all-knowing where He understands what we need to progress. (1:41) MH (1:07 seconds)

==

"The Father spoke one word for all eternity,

and He spoke it in silence,

and it is in silence that we hear it."

St. John of the Cross

==

We live in a society that's got a lot of noise. Listen to yourself and see what yourself is saying. Take time out. There are so many people that don't take time out. Some people can't even go to sleep unless the music is playing. They can't go to sleep unless the television is on. And there's noise everywhere, so shut it down. Once you shut it down you're going to hear something inside yourself. You have something talking within you. (3:38) MUH (23 seconds)

God will use anything and everything to reach out to us. God always is. God's always trying to connect with us. We forget that. We think, "Oh, I have to go and find God." But, in fact, it's more like opening our eyes to what's already there. God is reaching out to us all the time. (4:06) STA (15 seconds)

It's a lot like tuning your radio. Like when you're in a rural area and you're trying to find something to listen to and you're either pressing the digital thing or turning the dial trying to find a radio station - then you get some terrible country-western thing. You're searching, searching, searching for something good to listen to -

then finally you found it, and you fine tune your radio just so you get it.

You got to seek God - and there's a lot of voices out there like - "Chase the ladies; Get more money; Grow more hair; Have flat abdominal muscles so you'll be desirable to chicks" - whatever - there are all these voices out there booming at you all the time, telling you all this like crazy and often stupid stuff - and it's bad stuff. And so to tune in God, which is always the voice of love and kindness and peace and hope and joy - that's how you recognize it, because that's what it sounds like - when you get to that voice and then to be able to focus on it. And the thing that's not so hard is it's there - and if you contemplate love, contemplate goodness - you can find it. (2:20) PS (1:20 seconds)

I seek to be with God in praying; I seek to be with God in hanging around with Him and those who nobody else will have anything to do with; I seek to be with God through the sacraments in a wonderful way; I seek to be with God through doing what is right, through working for justice. So there are all kinds of ways I seek to be with God, but at the base of it all is shutting up and letting him talk to me. (MM) (29 seconds)

We all have guardian angels, we all have forces around us that are trying to lead us towards the good, but we've blocked it all out with noise, with sin, with vice, with just certain ways of thinking - so they can't reach us. We have to re-open the channel so that God can show us what He put us here to do - and if we do that He will show us and it becomes really easy because He does show you every step of the way. (1:17) MH (29 seconds)

If you get quiet and say, "God, what do I need to do?" God will let you know, but it's not necessarily in a big Charlton Heston booming voice broadcast. It's more in the Elijah sense - in the small, still inner voice. You just contemplate something and then you know that you know that you know. (2:20) PS (32 seconds)

===

"Spiritual reading is essential to the spiritual life."

Saint Padre Pio

===

When my journey began Jesus came to me and He said it was time for my purification and He said, "Gather the ancient sacred texts and all the ancient prayer books because you're going to learn from them." And He took me through - I didn't even know what they were - He showed me and He told me - He would give me these strange names, like the Holy Teaching of Vimalakirti - I was like, "How am I going to find that?" (23 seconds)

But I went through this process and He would tell me what to look for. One was the Dialogues of St. Catherine of Siena - which explains Christian mysticism and redemption in such a way that it remains my favorite books to this day. I really loved the writings, and was led to read the writings of Imam Ghazali - who is one of the mystical theologians of Islam - he wrote a really great text called the Ihya Ulumuddin - and I actually ordered that from overseas. And it's interesting because I compared that with the Catholic contemporary which is Father Adolf Tanqueray's The Spiritual Life - A Treatise On Ascetical And Mystical Theology - and it's so interesting when you look at the two and you look at many of these things - because there's some Jewish books that I'd like to mention as well - that they're just like different sides of the same coin. There might be a few different terms used but it's the same idea - they go through the purification of the soul through the virtues. (1:32) MH (1:07 seconds)

=================================

"Beauty without virtue is like a rose without scent."

Proverb

=================================

So what are the seven deadly sins? They are gluttony, lust, greed, pride, sloth, vanity, and avarice. (7 seconds)

And the seven virtues which counterbalance the seven deadly sins would be prudence, justice, fortitude, temperance, and faith, hope, and love - and love is also charity - and faith, hope, and love are in the area that's considered supernatural virtues, as well. (14 seconds)

If you want to talk about how to attain to the virtues and to discard some of the vices, you have to really take a close self-examination of yourself - and spiritual reading is one of the ways that you do this because that's how you make yourself aware of things - because many of the vices we have are so habitual that we would never see it in ourselves - we might see in someone else but not in ourselves. So in order to attain those virtues you want to engage in the spiritual reading, the prayer, and the meditation - but then you also have to practice the virtues that are opposite to the vices that you know you have. (37 seconds)

Let's say, for instance, you have an issue with lust… you're going to need some temperance. If you have a problem with greed, you're going to need to experience the virtue of justice in order to be more willing to part with your goods. (1:03) MH (16 seconds)

If you have a vice of greed, then you have to become mindful of that and you have to give. Greedy people don't like to give. So if you turn it around and you start giving, you can loosen that up a bit, and the hope will be that at some point you're no longer that greedy type person because you're giving. If it's gluttony, again, you have to back off from the table. (3:43) MUH (27 seconds)

For those of us who, when we start realizing that we have some failings - because I've had a lot - and I have been shown all of them and I'm sure there's more to come - when you see them there's a tendency to feel ashamed of yourself. (17 seconds)

I'll never forget the moment when I got to see my vanity through the eyes of God. It was so profoundly humbling in the sense of I saw vanity in all its ugliness. Everything I had ever done up to that point in my life - including the things that were good - were all done for the wrong reason - because they all had some kind of self-serving reason behind it.

Whether it's to make you do something good for someone else to make yourself to feel better - or you do something that's good but you're doing it because it'll make you look good - you do, whatever it is, some kind of self-serving reason. (40 seconds)

That was really a big turning point for me - it took me about a month to recover from it. And I have been told many times by my angels in the spirit, "This is a time we want you to apply Buddhist principles because otherwise we're going to waste too much time with you in shame, where we want you to understand this as a fetter - this is something holding you back."

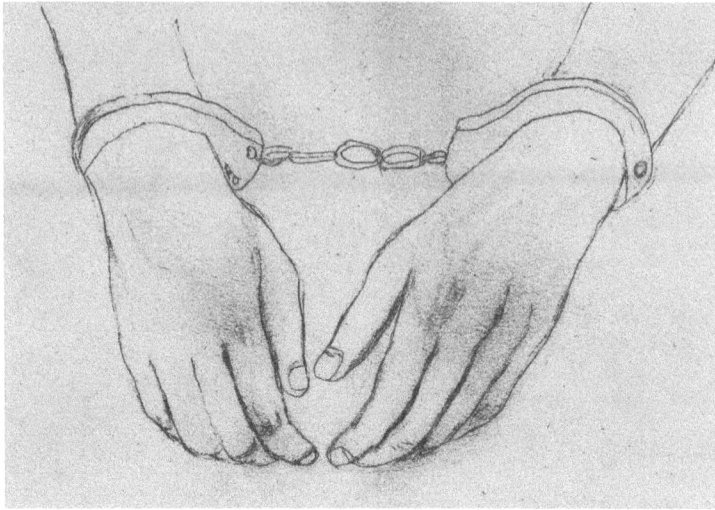

Christianity has it right - it's very correct - it's just that Buddhism takes it more from an intellectual standpoint - and that makes it a little quicker - because rather than spending a lot of time thinking about how ashamed we are of what we've done - we say, well, this is a fetter - this is a hindrance - this is keeping me from moving up towards the love that is God - so I'm going to let these things fall away. (1:50) MH (53 seconds)

When the Bhagavad Gita, like other Hindu texts, talks about this yogic practice of simplifying our lives, focusing, getting our bodies in order, our morality in order, our spiritual practice in order, it can at first sound very complicated; it can sound as if there's so many things to do. But, generally speaking, it really is an effort to stop doing things, stop worrying about things, stop needing things - physically, mentally, psychologically - coming into a simpler and simpler state where one is confronting and being confronted by ultimate reality.

And because traditions like that of Hinduism and the Bhagavad Gita believe that one finds one's joy in the presence of the Divine, ultimately being happy, rejoicing in life, finding peace, come down to uncluttering one's life, doing away with the things that stand in our way and our obstacles and coming to that simple presence of ourselves and the Divine. Once one gets there, this is what we are made for, this is who we are. And in that moment, we find the joy of our life, we find the bliss - and there's no reason ever to leave that condition. (3:19) CL (1:15 seconds)

```
==================================
```
"No servant can serve two masters."

Luke 16:13
```
==================================
```

The difficult most difficult part of my experience was not the hellish part that I experienced to get to the good part - that was insignificant compared to what Jesus told me about God's disappointment with this world because it's a whole lot bigger than me. The human race has failed miserably in what God's hope and expectation was what we can be. Granted, God put us in a very challenging world - this world is not easy. But the world that God wants - and that God will get in the future - it's going to happen because it's what God wants, and God gets what God wants - one way or another - that world is going to come about and it's so different than the world we have. (51 seconds)

God doesn't like the idea of propelling bits of metal through exploding gases into each other's guts to prove that you're right and they're wrong. (10 seconds)

God doesn't like the idea that a small portion of the planet has so much resources and meanwhile there are people in the world who literally don't have enough to eat, don't have enough clothes to wear, don't have enough shelter to keep themselves dry when it rains. They don't have the minimal resources for survival. And when they show those miserable pictures of them on T.V. - it's like, "Change the channel - don't bore me with the starving children." (2:23) PS (29 seconds)

I remember I went to a church to speak many years ago and the pastor told me that he has a problem with his congregation because they're rich - and because they're rich they don't believe they commit sin. So it's a challenge for him to teach them certain things because they think, "Oh, I don't do that." But no, they can do it just like anybody else. MUH (54:00) (24 seconds)

We don't realize how dumb it is that we focus so much on mortal, impermanent things in this world. We focus on how we look on the outside, whether or not we have enough degrees, whether or not we make enough money - and you know the only thing that matters when you're on that deathbed is the people you love and whether or not you loved well - whether or not you actually improved and progressed in your spiritual life - if you moved closer to God rather than further away. (1:01) MH (35 seconds)

People who want more and more things are trying to make up for an inner feeling of inadequacy and unfulfillment by piling on outer things, but it never works, right? And then as they do that, they get angry with others because they think that... they want to take things from other people – so they imagine that other people want to take things from them. (2:49) TH (19 seconds)

Living from your center, knowing who you are, having a sense that you are living what God created you to live is a pearl of great price, and it can't be bought and no one or nothing can take it away from you. Careers come and go. Money can come and go. There's nothing wrong with money - money can do great things - but it's a poor master. It's a great tool - terrible master. We need more to ground our sense of worth than money. When people live too far from their center, you can tell because they're always looking to be entertained and distracted from the emptiness they find inside. (4:01) STA (39 seconds)

The Buddhist legend of coming to the guide and saying, "I'm suffering - I can't deal with it." "Okay, well, I want to help you. This is what you do - go find a home that has known no suffering." So the person goes off to the home and says, "I'm looking for a home where there's no suffering." "Oh, no, that's not here," tells him all the suffering, and the person starts working with them - then goes to the next home, same thing - works with them - before they know it, they forget about their own suffering. (2:37) RM (22 seconds)

As the Dalai Lama says, "If you want to be happier yourself then make other people happy, and forget about being happy yourself." Because as long as you're worried about being happy yourself, you'll be unhappy - because you'll measure how happy you are and then you'll not think it's happy enough. You'll want another ice cream cone, you'll want another extra thing. But if you forget about how happy you are and you're just trying to make another person happy, then without even trying you'll be happy. So as the Dalai Lama says, "If you're going to be selfish seeking your own happiness, at least be a wise selfish and affect other being's happiness." (2:51) TH (36 seconds)

Good deeds done well encourage more good deeds done well. A lot of these kinds of things we don't realize the astronomical effect it has when we try to bring God into what we are doing and we try to keep in mind the well-being of everyone involved and everyone around us - that others mimic and they start doing the same. And so it multiplies - and you bring more and more light into this world. (1:54) MH (32 seconds)

Every time there's an act of goodness - of bringing God's light in the world - you're bringing healing. There's a wonderful traditional phrase in Jewish mysticism - it's very much used in normative Jewish practice today - it's Tikkun Olam. Literally, it means to repair the world. The acts that we can do on a daily basis that help bring healing to the world. You're not commanded by God to fix everything, but you are commanded by God to keep trying. (2:34) RM (29 seconds)

======================================

"Love thy neighbor as thyself."

Leviticus 19:18

======================================

When Jesus told me that my fate was to come back in this world and that I was not going to go to heaven - which is what I wanted to - I argued as forcibly as I could to not send me back here. I told Him that the world was full of evil - it was a terrible place. And He said, "Yeah, there's a lot of evil in the world and there's a lot of bad stuff in the world, but there's a lot of good and a lot of loving people." And He said that "What you are in your heart is what you're going to seek. If you seek hate, you will find hate, and you are hate. If you seek love, you'll find love and you'll be love. If you seek kindness you'll find kindness, and you'll be kindness." And so we have to be it, and seek it, and then we will find it.

So I said, "But what's the point of sending me back? Why would you want me to go back to that world? If you really loved me you wouldn't send me back to that place." And He said, "I need you. I need you back there." I said, "You need me to do what?" And He said, "I need you to change the world." I said, "Whoa, whoa, whoa - I'm not going to change the world!" I said, "I don't even know if I could change me! I don't know if I can be what you want me to be - be the loving, kind person you want me to be - and asking me to be the Savior of the world…" He didn't say that, I said it - I was sort of exaggerating my role. He said, "No, that's really what I want you to do. I want you to change the world."

"That's crazy," I said. "People that try and change the world come out to a bad end. We're talking about Stalin and Hitler and Genghis Khan - they all wanted to change the world and they were all megalomaniacs. I don't want to go back and be a megalomaniac." He said, "No, no, no - you got it all wrong - they were bad, they were megalomaniacs. That's not how I want you to change the world." And I said, "Well, how do want me to change the world?" He said, "Love somebody." And I said, "Okay… but what's the rest of the plan?" He said, "No, that's the whole plan." And I said, "If I go back and love someone - that changes the world?" And He said, "That's the plan. That's it." I said, "What's the rest of the plan!!?" He said, "That's the whole plan - there is no more - just love somebody." And I said, "If I love somebody - how in the world will that change anything?" And He said, "If you love someone - really truly love them - they will love someone - and that person will love someone - and that person will love someone."

And me, being a clever fellow I was, I said, "Yeah - and then they get run over by a truck and that's the end of the plan." And He said, "No… because I never said you're the only one." He said, "There's a lot." And I said, "Well, how many?" He said, "Millions. Millions of people are the instrument of change." And I said, "Okay, but there are a lot of trucks down there and a lot of bad stuff can happen to thwart the millions of people trying to love somebody." And He said, "Yeah, but I have a backup." I said, "What's the backup?" And He said, "Angels." And I said, "So you're going to bring the angels into this?" And He said, "The angels are already in it - they're already intervening." He said, "So I got millions of people, I got angels beyond counting all trying to inspire people, encourage people, help people." He said, "This is God's Will - it is inevitable - it's going to happen one way or another. It has to happen because it's what God wants."

And I said, "Well when you put it that way - when you put it as like God's going to make it happen - sure, I'd be happy to be part of it!"

So anyways, this is my interpretation: You're either part of the program or you're against it. There is no longer an opportunity to sit on the fence and say, "Oh, look at the foolish loving people doing the loving thing - good luck to them and the Boston Red Sox; and look at the bad people going around in a fermenting hate and fear and strife in the world - good luck to them." You can't do that anymore - you're either in the program, which is God's program of turning this world into a loving and kind place, or you're against the program. And there's nothing in between. (2:29) PS (4:34 seconds)

==================================

==================================

We are told that you cannot even go to sleep if your neighbor's hungry and you have food. The Prophet Muhammad, peace be upon him, told us that our neighbors are forty houses in front of us, forty houses in back of us, and forty houses on the side of us. And he told us that he received so many instructions from Almighty about the neighbor that he thought that the neighbor was going to actually be in the will - that you have to actually put the neighbor in the will. So he told us to treat our neighbor as we treat ourselves. (3:34) MUH (29 seconds)

How do I love God in this life? I don't do it by putting on all kinds of fancy clothes with jewels and standing and waving my hand and saying, "I love God." I don't do it by standing in a pulpit and saying, "I love God." I don't do it by wearing a button that says, "I love God and He loves me." I do it by going to the soup kitchen down the street. I do it by buying a coat for the guy I know is cold. I do it by taking care of those who are the most broken in life and loving them. How do you get to heaven? By loving God - and by loving Him in my neighbor. (MM) (38 seconds)

We can't journey back to God without taking into account our obligation to our neighbor. It's not just about me and God. It's about me and the whole human community and how together this earth can be more like the kingdom of God - which is a community of justice, of love, of peace. No one's God says, "Hate your neighbor." (20 seconds)

Some fanatics in every religion distort, perhaps, but rightly understood the core of all religions is a journey of love. A journey toward our fellow human beings and toward God not away from them. (3:47) STA (12 seconds)

A lot of the times God is saying, "Just *be*. Just be there with that person. You don't you have to fix them - they're not broken. If they got brokenness, I'll fix them - you just love them the way they are - just love them the way they are." I've been with drug users, prostitutes, alcoholics, murderers - I did a ministry with a guy on death row for a long time - and God was saying, "You don't have to preach to these people - just love them. I'll take care of the rest." (2:13) PS (31 seconds)

Love your neighbor as yourself - everything else is commentary. If you're really serious about that, you're starting in a position of love. If everyone just started with that - that one thing - imagine how different the world would be. "I love you. Now let's talk." (2:36) RM (15 seconds)

=================================

Epilogue

=================================

In the Hindu religious traditions there is a very universal sense that we are all on the path, and that all beings are destined toward a higher development, toward true knowledge, toward ultimately bliss, in union with the ultimate reality, or as that reality, or with God. And I think the good Hindu teacher can see a crowd before her or him and realize that each person here is on the spiritual path, has the same destiny, and yet needs to be allowed to travel at his or her own pace. And trying to make somebody travel at somebody else's pace and speed things up or slow things down only leads to unhappiness for everyone. So everyone is on the journey and yet people are at different stages, just as we tend to be at different stages of life depending on our age or circumstances. (3:30) CL (49 seconds)

The goal for all of us is that we're trying to get to God - and the only way we can do that is by becoming more and more holy. Does that mean that any of us are going to achieve perfection in this life? No... but we can become more aware and even just having the humility to realize who we really are in relation to God is a really good place to start. (1:22) MH (24 seconds)

I feel that as we are trying to move forward and I think that the church is trying to recognize the fact that they need to open up and change some of their old methods. I feel that a lot of them were looking at it from the perspective that devils and demons and these things were something from the stone ages and it really didn't encompass our world. (3:02) JZ (26 seconds)

The book of Revelation is a very unique piece of literature because it's a kind of a literature - apocalyptic literature - that was very popular in those years immediately after the death and resurrection of Christ in the early days of the church - and it was not necessarily meant as a prediction of the way things are going to happen in a physical, historical way. So to say that, in effect, we each participate in our own kind of cosmic battle - our own internal battle between light and darkness - well, that's the theme of everything I've saying along the way - it's true. And so one can see this kind of cosmic battle as simply being a description of what's going on inside of each of us. (MM) (48 seconds)

I think the very idea of the end of the world is one of those concepts that we have in mind without ever really knowing what to make of it in terms of history. We do have a sense that everything ends - summer ends, winter ends, the day ends. We know through the experience of death that so many people we love... their lives come to an end. And I think we can expand that and say the world, too, will come to an end. It may be that the Armageddon or the Last Judgment matters most in terms of my life, my facing up to my destiny, my facing up to the fact that some day this life will be over and there are basic choices to be made about to live in the face of that reality. (3:27) CL (46 seconds)

Judgment is a little different than people think because people think of Judgment as like an external group or individual saying, "You're good, you're bad." That's not the way it works - our Judgment is what our hearts are. When I had my life review - I could summarize my life review simply by saying I was judged entirely by the quality of my relationships - of whether my relationships were loving and caring and compassionate and kind, or whether my relationships with other people were me being manipulative and greedy and self-centered. And, unfortunately, I was the latter and not the former. (1:59) PS (46 seconds)

One of the biggest issues that I see in the world today is too many people not realizing that there is a function and a purpose for us being here - and that function was told to me in a near-death experience I had with Jesus Christ - and it's very simple: We're supposed to go from selfishness to selflessness. (1:57) MH (22 seconds)

==

==

for more information visit

www.theroadtoarmageddon.com

www.ingramcontent.com/pod-product-compliance
Lightning Source LLC
Chambersburg PA
CBHW060702030426
42337CB00017B/2728